Whispers Of My Soul

Deepali Jain Agrawal

BookLeaf Publishing

India | USA | UK

Presentation by *BookLeaf Publishing*

Web: www.bookleafpub.com

E-mail: info@bookleafpub.com

ISBN: 9789363305885

First edition 2024

I dedicate this book to all those lovely souls out there who aspire to achieve something new everyday with fighting their own battles within and still rising up high for a new challenge.

ACKNOWLEDGEMENT

To my angel in heaven, Dad I can feel your presence deep inside my soul and you have proved the essence of my book, that soul is eternal.

My kids, family, friends and loved ones without whose support and love i wouldn't have walked so far.

Last but not the least,
My sister and my soulmate my husband thank you and I love you.

PREFACE

After the success of my first 2 books, "Shine on a Moonlit Path" and "If Heart Could Speak", I was unsure if I felt the need to write more, or if I needed a break. However, I was then blessed, earning a 21st Century Emily Dickinson award on my 2nd book. Right then my soul whispered its true desire. So, after long hours of work, dedication, happiness, sadness, and MANY more emotions, this book was born. I am proud to present to you, with even deeper meanings, and stronger emotions, "Whispers of My Soul".

Whispers of the wind

Whisper of the wind soft and light,
Carrying secrets of your day so bright.
A calm touch on the cheek,
Whispering through a language where mysteries
speak.

To the distant land where horizon meet,
To the mountain peak high to valley so deep.
The wind which travels freely without care,
carrying messages of love so fair.

Listen closely to its gentle sign,
A melody sung beneath the sky.
For in this moment we release,
An enchanting moment of our inner peace.

Oh whispers of the wind so kind,
Embrace us in your solace so peaceful we find.
Carry us a far on your wings for a gentle flight,
Piercing through a tiring day into a calm night.

Breeze

In the morning hush,
Soft cool air touches your tender skin,
Caressing and teasing with a cool essence,
Reminding you of nature's new dawn in a tease.

Leaves rustling and swaying away,
Birds chirping and singing away in harmony,
Gentle breeze carrying a soft fragrance,
Reminding us of a new day blossoming like a
flower.

As the dusk makes it way.
Day's stress melts away.
Embracing yourself in a calm hug,
A gentle breeze engulf you in a sweet night
snug.

Waves

Born from the ocean's vast appear,
Where the sky and sea embrace in dance,
A rhythmic move forms an enormous wave,
Telling tales of a timeless phase.

Born from the essence of winds that plays
around,
It rises up as high and crashing away,
A crest of foam a rise of dream,
Merging the hopes of day and night.

With every crest that sway up high,
And every sound that softly cries,
Every wave creates a timeless tale,
Stories of strength, beauty, hopes and fame.

Yet it happily dance upon the sea,
Every wave without fail reflects our destiny,
Never to stop trying to raise to reach the shore,
A lesson for life is taught by every trying mighty
wave.

Seaside

Walking by the seaside where waves embrace,
Sand shine in the awe of warm sun grace.
Seagulls flying diving for a treat,
Dancing and flapping around for happy greet.

Crashing waves fierce and low,
Singing ocean's song both bold and slow.
Unfolding tales of boundless sea,
Engulfing secrets shared while walking hand in
hand.

Horizons kiss where sky meets the tide,
Holds dreams and hopes in its embrace wide.
The sand a canvas warm and gold,
Engraving secrets of the deep untold.

Waves
Born from the ocean's vast appear,
Where the sky and sea embrace in dance,
A rhythmic move forms an enormous wave,
Telling tales of a timeless phase

Footprints

Soft and deep prints in the sand,
Marks the place where dreams expand.
Each step portray a story brief yet bright,
Etched deep in heart over the time.
Footprints fades with tide's embrace,
It leaves a trace full of loving grace.
Future upholding wet emotions,
Which were wash away and securely stored
away in the ocean's chest.

Soul

In the depth of our body where breath stay,
The soul's. essence truly find its way.
An eternal flame that enlighten the body,
A selfless guiding star strong like nobody.

Through joy or any bitter strife,
It cuts through the sorrow with honey dipped
knife.
In midst of dilemma or silence,
It whispers calm notes which only heart can
recognize.

An invincible warrior of human body,
A forever sacred song, your inner self best friend
like nobody.

Finally

I am not angry anymore,
Finally I chose to move on.
I buried all the grudges and hurt,
I feel heavy carrying them afar.
The strength in me motivated me to move
forward,
I couldn't take it all anymore,
The damage was weighing me down.
I carried the remaining pieces with me,
I packed them safely in the safe of my chest and
I moved on finally……

Chirping of Love

As the morning dew yawns at the dawn,
Singing of melodious birds fill the lawn.
A ray of hope and destiny begin,
Giving your dreams wings to fly again.

Chirping and singing all over again,
Songs of praise and melody of fame.
Engulfing a whole new day in a singing way,
Heart beat is the only rhythm, to take you afloat
away.

Self Love

I started to love myself,
I may not be perfect,
But i am who I am.
Full of love and gratitude,
Flaws I may have but pure intentions is who I
am.

Embracing myself with warm hug,
Cheers to myself for coming up so far.
In the end when you look inside,
A smile so enchanting and pure awaits,
To welcome your true soul which is residing
inside.

Sunrise

In the still of morning grace,
A dawn of light paints the sky's embrace.
Golden paint engulf the dark flight,
Warding off the dark starry night.

A new dream begins to unfold,
As the dawn's first light begins to offload.
A ray of hope and aspire to chase what's lost,
Reborn in the golden hour of the day at a gentle cost.

Attachment

A love so pure and naive,
Seeking care and touch of pure play.
Always giving never reluctant,
Finding solace in pure peace portray.

Attachment an unnecessary emotion,
Giving away unintentionally is a pure
requirement.
Hurt, rejection, unfulfilled desires,
My detachment through my soul is my only pure
attachment.

Soulmate

Connection of a soul to another,
Understanding and calmness just to be with one
and another.
Making imperfection as a weapon,
To cut through life challenges and evolve as one
perfect winner.
Soulmate seems a very small word,
In it contains a vast unending pieces of
connection.
Like a puzzle is not complete even if a piece
goes missing,
You my mate is an important part of my soulful
puzzle,
My most important last piece of an incomplete
puzzle.

Move On

Feeling drowned and hurt,
Pulling down by pain and its dirt.

Clinging onto grudges making me feeble,
Holding me strong not to move on.

Taking revenge is like paying a huge fee,
Forgive and forget is the golden key.

Challenge is not to stress and keep on going,
But to accept the change and embrace it
gracefully.

Let the Karma play its game,
End of the day inner peace is the only fame.

Start afresh, shed the past in the bin,
Get on your feet, face the sun with a beautiful
grin.

Dreams

In the quiet dawn of night,
When your eyes are sleepy in the dim light.
Tiptoe of a sweet quiet tipsy toe dance,
Woven with hopes a dream is woven in a glance.
Stars being the only light in the sky,
Giving your dreams, wings to fly.
Whispers of tomorrow in twilight sea,
Creating waves where hearts can float free.
In the labyrinth of sleep, where souls play,
We hide and seek the visions which drift away.
Every dream a glimpse and hope of divine,
Woven with a secret story solely yours and
mine.
As the morning light makes it way,
A sweet little linger taste of dream remains, as
rest fades away.

Love

15

In your eyes lie the infinite mysteries,
So vast creating our million unspoken stories.
A simple touch a deep kiss,
In that moment lies endless bliss.
Love at first sight as it say,
In your embrace my unspoken dreams lay.
A touch a smile a whispered song,
In your warm heart is where I belong.

Soul Friend

In a world full of strangers a friendly smile,
You are the echo a perfect sign.
A soul friend found through time and grace,
In every glance as we embrace.

Our laughter creating positive vibes,
A bond that turns the dark to light.
Your presence makes my spirit soar,
Together we can unlock any eye's doors.

Through this roller coaster kind of life,
A sense of security cutting the strife.
Path of journey both wild and grand,
I'm glad I have you to hold on my soul friend.

Echoes of our Heart

In quiet corners of the mind,
Where the soul whispers silently like a chime.
Memories faint, soft yet so clear,
Echoes of yester years we hold dear.

Time passes, seasons change,
Moments once lived never fade.
Like on a cold freezing night,
They engulf our soul like a warm light.

In laughter's glow, or tearful's sighs,
In every glance or sad goodbyes.
They paint our lives with moments so bright,
A series of wrongs or rights.
Cheers to our loved ones in our spirits,
A smile on our face to welcome new memories
so very bright.

Crossroad

At the crossroad of life where paths entwine,
A dilemma dances, baffled with signs.
Two roads diverge one steep one small,
A choice to make, a heart's sweet call.

Each path has its crawl,
One promising rise, the other a tough fall.
Future whispers close in ears,
A fear, a dilemma covers the mind not so clear.

The mind debates, the heart stands still,
Caught between a saga of emptiness to fill.
A step forward, or a step back,
Confusion to move forward on life's track.

In the shadows of dark, or bright light,
The decision is yours, wrong or right.
No map to guide, no compass so true,
Choice is yours, even when all turns blue.

Conquer the doubt, let courageous intentions
win,
For in the battle, your true self will emerge from
within.

At the journey of crossroads, where streets
entwine,
Trust your instincts for the way, in the end, the
path will shine.

Within

I want to love you from my soul,
For my heart may die,
Or my mind might forget,
But in the end noting but my soul would
ever stay eternal and pure as a God's will desire.

Spread your Wings

A new beginning a new era so bright,
Spread your wings, take your flight.
Beyond the clouds, beyond the blue,
Seek your dreams that call you.

A gush of wind to hold your grace,
Soar up high, embrace your inner place.
In the vast sky so blue and clear,
Spread your wings and conquer the horizon with
no fear.

Whispers of my Soul

In the midst of crowd hear my voice so clear,
Don't be scared of the struggle in the fight of
fear.
For your heart or mind might fail to recognize,
Listen carefully to your inner self as in it,
resides the whispers of my soul,
So pure and bright.